The Super Simple Home Buyer's Handbook

Timothy L Carver & Clint T Carver

Table of Contents

Introduction

Avoiding a Nightmare House

Not long ago we talked with a couple who described their first home as "a nightmare."

"We never should have purchased that home," they said. "We had no clue what we were doing and no idea about all the problems the home had. We've spent thousands in repairs."

Unfortunately, that experience is not uncommon. There are many "moving parts" in the home buying process that can cause uninformed people to make serious and costly mistakes.

Even those who have purchased a previous home can stumble.

A Simpler Approach

There are numerous good books on the market that offer a large amount of helpful information about buying a home. Most are long and detailed.

Ours is a *bare-bones* approach. We don't try to explain EVERYTHING. We want to share the MOST CRITICAL tips that will save you money, time and help you avoid costly mistakes.

Our Background

Our expertise encompasses both the *mortgage and real estate worlds,* and our experiences have given us many valuable insights that we want to share.

In addition, we have experience in *construction and remodeling*, which gives us the ability to help clients spot excellent vs. poor workmanship.

So dive in! Learn lots! You can also visit our website for more FREE ideas!

www.MonsterHomeBuyerHelps.com

CHAPTER 1

The Step-by-Step Checklist

The Step-by-Step Process of Buying a Home

1. ☐ **Check Your Credit Score**

   a. Get a free credit report:
      https://www.annualcreditreport.com/index.action

   b. Go to the *Helpful Resources* of this book for tips in raising your credit score.

2. ☐ **Select a Lender**

   a. Get quotes from at least 3 different lenders.

   b. Obtain a pre-approval letter from your lender.

3. ☐ **Complete Your Wish List**

4. ☐ **Select a Real Estate Agent**

   a. Get suggestions from family and friends.

b.   Read online reviews.

c.   Call or meet with potential agents.

5.   ☐ **Share Information with Your Agent**

a.   Share your pre-approval letter.

b.   Share your Wish List with your agent.

6.   ☐ **Look at Homes Online**

a.   Home-searching websites you may find helpful:

- *Realtor.com*
- *Redfin.com*
- *Zillow.com*
- *Homes.com*

7.   ☐ **Select Homes You Want to Tour**

a.   Your real estate agent will set up these appointments for you.

b.   Expect to see approximately two homes per hour.

8.   ☐ **Make an Offer**

a.   Obtain a Cost Market Analysis (see *Definitions*) from your real estate agent to help determine the current value of the home you are considering.

b.   Work with your real estate agent to write an offer and submit it to the seller's agent.

c.   Work through your agent on counter-offers and any further negotiations.

9. ☐ **Pay the Earnest Money (see *Definitions*)**

    a. Give your earnest money to your agent's broker. Your agent will help with this.

10. ☐ **Read the Seller Disclosures (see *Definitions*)**

    a. Review the Seller Disclosures that your agent gives you from the seller's agent.

    b. Discuss concerns with your agent.

11. ☐ **Set Up the Inspection**

    a. Read online reviews to help select an inspection company.

    b. Set a date for the home inspection. The inspector will usually work with the seller's agent to arrange a time.

    c. Meet with the inspector at the conclusion of the inspection to discuss and observe any concerns he wants to point out.

    d. The inspector will send you and your agent a printed/electronic copy of the inspection.

    e. Discuss any concerns with your agent.

12. ☐ **Determine Repair Requests**

    a. Ask your real estate agent to help with repair requests, if necessary.

13. ☐ **Obtain the Appraisal**

   a. Your lender will arrange for an appraisal to determine if the home "comes in at-value," (if it's worth at least as much as the offered purchase price).

   b. Obtain the results of the appraisal from the lender.

14. ☐ **Select a Home Warranty Policy**

   a. Check with your agent and online reviews to find a reliable home warranty company.

      • The seller usually agrees in the contract to pay for the home warranty policy.

      • The seller usually sets the amount for the home warranty, but this can be negotiated.

      • The buyer should be allowed to select the warranty company.

15. ☐ **Select a Title Company (see *Definitions*)**

   a. Select a title company from reviews online or get suggestions from your agent.

16. ☐ **Schedule the Move**

   a. Schedule the move several weeks prior to your actual move.

   b. Contact family and friends to help or hire professional movers.

17. ☐ Arrange for the Utilities

    a. Change the utilities (gas, electricity, water, sewer, trash) to your name. Do this prior to the owners turning their utilities off and you'll save yourself a re-connect fee.

    b. Contact the utilities to determine their policies. Most utilities will allow you to put the service in your name with just a phone call. Some require a copy of the closing statement that you receive at settlement.

18. ☐ Settlement and Closing (see *Definitions*)

    a. Ask your agent to arrange a date and time with you and the title company.

    b. Settlement is where you sign final documents and payments are wired. This is usually done in the office of the title company. The title company handles wiring the money.

    c. Be sure to discuss with your agent the danger of wire fraud.

    d. Closing and funding take place when documents are recorded and the payment is received. Both usually happen a day after settlement.

19. ☐ Welcome Home!

    a. Meet your agent at your new home to receive your keys!

    b. Don't forget to get the garage door openers from your agent also.

You may want to change your garage door code for safety reasons.

CHAPTER 2

The Wish List

What Are You Looking for in a Home?

This is a great place to start. But <u>don't forget</u> that most of what you can realistically purchase in a home will be determined by what you can afford.

Make sure you meet with a lender BEFORE you get too focused on what you're looking for. Lenders will review your credit and earnings and then determine the amount they are willing to lend you.

We know clients who had to revamp their wish list because they made their list before consulting a lender. Their wishes turned out to be larger than their loan.

And don't forget that you'll need money for a down payment and closing costs (see *Definitions*).

Share your answers to the eight questions below with your real estate agent. Your answers will help him/her zero in on what you're looking for.

1. What is the maximum amount you have been approved for?

2. How much down payment do you have?

3. What type of loan will you get (cash, conventional, FHA, VA)?

4. Are you okay with a short sale (see *Definitions*)?

5. Would you consider a "fixer upper?"

   a. I want the home ready to move in

   b. I would be willing to do some fix-up work

   c. I would be willing to do a lot of fix up work

6. What style of home do you prefer?

   a. One level

   b. Two levels

   c. Town house/condo

7. What counties and cities are you considering?

8. List any additional information that would be helpful for your real estate agent.

Use the chart below to identify your priorities when choosing your home:

	Must Have	Nice to Have	Doesn't Matter
Age of Home			
HOA			
Garage			
Number of Bedrooms			
Number of Bathrooms			
Basement			
Fenced Yard			
Patio/Deck			
RV Parking			
Air Conditioning			
Other			
Other			
Other			

CHAPTER 3

The Definite Do's

These Tips Will Save You MONEY and SORROW!

Start Saving ASAP!

Almost all mortgage lenders will require a down payment from you.

But contrary to popular belief, you don't need 20% down. The minimum down payment you will need to buy a home with an FHA loan is 3.5% of the loan amount. A conventional loan usually requires a down payment of 5% of the amount of the loan.

On top of your down payment, you'll need to have enough money for your closing costs (see *Definitions*). Closing costs usually amount to about 3% of the price of the home.

Saving that much money may take you awhile, so you can't start too soon.

Watch for ways you can cut back on expenses. It may not be as hard as you think. Here are several ways that you can add to your bank account fairly quickly:

- Have a portion of your pay check deposited in your savings account each month.

- Pay off your credit cards or keep the balance under 30% of your limit.

- Don't buy a new car. New cars are not a good investment. Buy a good used one that you can pay cash for, if possible. You'll save hundreds each month.

- Who said there's no free lunch? There is if you bring lunch from home. Restaurant lunches these days cost at least $5 to $10. Multiply that by 20 working days in a month and you'll find that's at least $100 per month. Bring your lunch from home and save over $1,000 in a year!

- Cut the cable costs and save more than $100 each month.

- Cut back your spending on new clothes and vacations for a while. Definitely worth it!

Improve Your Credit Score

Lenders don't get excited about loaning money to people with poor credit. So they charge them higher interest rates. Want the best interest rate possible? A great credit score will help tremendously. Most lenders want a minimum of 640 but having a credit score of 720 will help you get a lower interest rate.

Get Pre-Qualified *Before* You Start Home Shopping

You can't determine how much home you can buy until you know how much money you qualify to borrow. A mortgage company can help you compute this. Once you are pre-qualified, you will receive a letter from the lender stating the loan amount you qualify for. Give the letter to your agent. The seller's agent will almost always want to know if you have been pre-qualified. And your agent may require you to be pre-qualified before he/she will begin showing you homes.

Get Interest Rate Quotes from at Least Three Lenders

Do all grocery stores offer the same prices on their products? Of course not. Similarly, banks and mortgage lenders vary in their programs and rates. Chat with at least three lenders to find the best deal for you. Let them know that you're getting other quotes as this may encourage them to lower their quote.

Talk with Both a Bank *and* a Mortgage Broker

Should you use a bank or a mortgage broker? Here are the advantages and disadvantages of each.

Bank Advantages:

- Banks use their own money to fund mortgages. They have their own loan officers, processors, underwriters, etc.

- Banks work on your loan from beginning to end. They may sometimes offer lower rates.

Bank Disadvantages:

- Banks typically offer fewer types of home loans.

- If they don't have the kind of loan that's best for you, they may not tell you about it.

Mortgage Broker Advantages:

- Brokers work with numerous banks, lenders and mortgage companies.

- Brokers shop around to various lenders to find the best interest rate and best loan product for your situation.

- You can apply for a mortgage with a broker, and they can shop and compare the mortgage options for you.

- Brokers may be able to arrange a mortgage for those having trouble getting approved by a bank, such as self-employed people and those with poor credit histories.

Mortgage Broker Disadvantages:

- Broker fees typically range from 0.5% to 1% of the mortgage.

Hire a Real Estate Agent

Our recommendation is to ALWAYS hire an agent to represent you—especially as the home buyer! The home <u>seller</u> almost always pays the commissions for both the seller's and the buyer's agent. Why not use the services of a real estate agent if there's no cost to you?

Here's what an agent will do for you:

- Find you a home that meets your needs with a price you can afford

- Set up appointments to visit the homes you would like to see

- Point out pros and cons of each home you walk through

- Create a Cost Market Analysis (see *Definitions*) to determine if the sales price matches what the home is worth

- Help you determine how much to offer on the home

- Help you fill out and submit the contract (Real Estate Purchase Contract – see *Definitions*)

- Help you negotiate the deal (Some agents are hesitant to negotiate. Make sure your agent is willing to negotiate for you.)

- Help you read and understand the Seller Disclosures (see *Definitions*)

- Set up the home inspection (see *Definitions*)

- Help you negotiate needed repairs with the seller

- Help you stay on track with contract deadlines

- Work with lender to make sure deadlines are met

- Whew! That's a ton of great services at no cost to you!

Check Out the Neighborhood

Knock on a few doors around any home you are considering. Ask neighbors if they like the area, the neighborhood, the schools, etc. You'll usually find people who are happy to talk with you. If you don't find friendly people who are willing to chat with you, that may tell you something about the neighborhood!

Also, look at the homes in the neighborhood. Are there any that would bring down the value of the home you're considering? One of our clients found a home he really liked and looked at the home across the street. It looked like an automobile junk yard. He decided to look elsewhere.

Negotiate the Deal

This is one of the best reasons to have a real estate agent. Most agents have access to software programs that help determine the value of the home. Use that information to help you negotiate the deal.

Most sellers start higher in their sales price because they know that most people want to negotiate. Many sellers expect you to negotiate. It doesn't hurt to ask for a better deal, unless there are multiple offers on the property. Your agent will help you and will represent you in the negotiations. But don't "low ball" (see *Definitions*) with your offer. We have seen buyers lose the sale because they started with a low ball offer. Try to think "win-win"!

Ask for Closing Costs

Ask the seller to pay "Closing Costs" (see *Definitions*). In a "seller's market" (see *Definitions*) they may not agree to do so, but it never hurts to ask. Your agent can help you with this.

Chapter 4

The Deadly Don'ts

Big "No-No's" That Can Cause Big Problems

Don't Rely on Online Mortgage Calculators

Mortgage calculators don't always include important components, such as homeowner's insurance, property taxes, and mortgage insurance. Sit down with a lender to get a more accurate number. We've had clients who used online calculators to determine what they could afford and then were deeply disappointed when they sat down with a lender and learned they qualified for MUCH less.

Don't Buy More House Than You Can Afford

Just because you can qualify for a $350,000 loan doesn't mean you can afford the monthly mortgage payments. The term "house poor" means you have sunk so much of your income into paying for your mortgage that you have little for anything else. Some experts say your house payment should be approximately 25% of your take-home pay. Others suggest you could go as high as 30%, as long as you have no other outstanding debt and don't plan to go into further debt.

Don't Expect to Find Your Dream House

If this is your first or even your second home, you probably won't get EVERYTHING on your Wish List. Maybe you can't afford a garage yet. That will come in time. Be patient. Shoot for getting the most important things on your list. Some buyers are so intent on getting everything on their list that they miss a good deal on a home.

Don't Buy a Fixer-Upper Unless . . .

We've known people who bought a fixer-upper home but had no do-it-yourself (DIY) skills. In the process of "fixing-it-up" they actually made the home worse and reduced its value. Seriously. And they ended up selling it for less than what they thought they could. However, if you have some good DIY skills – or are willing to learn – buying a fixer-upper might be a good idea. Just make sure you know what you're doing so you don't jump in over your head.

Avoid Big Purchases Prior to Closing

Mortgage lenders check your credit when you're being approved and again just before "closing" (see

Definitions). They want to make sure nothing has changed in your financial status. Big purchases can mess with your credit score and make your lender nervous. In addition, don't open new credit cards or create a new account with a furniture store. We've known buyers who have learned this lesson the hard way. Wait until the purchase has been finalized before you go shopping for bigger items! And avoid switching jobs when you're in the middle of buying a home.

CHAPTER 5

Top Home Touring Tips

What to Look for When Touring a Home

There are things that only an inspector will be able to spot on a house. ALWAYS get the home inspected before you buy it. But there are LOTS of things you can watch for that will give you significant insights into the home you are touring.

Stop at the Curb

After they've pulled up to the home and stepped out of the car, we teach our clients to take time to look around. Your home's value is affected by the homes around it. Pause to answer these questions:

- What is the condition of the neighboring homes?

- What do the yards look like in the neighborhood?

- Does anyone have piles of junk in their yard or three cars torn apart in the driveway?

- Are the homes in the neighborhood significantly older than the home you are looking at?

Up on the Housetop

Now before you walk into the house, look at the roof. It can be a MAJOR expense to replace a roof, so you'll want to find out what condition it's in. A good inspector will climb on your roof for a close look (unless it has ice or snow on it) and will take photos of any concerns. But there's quite a bit you can spot from the ground.

Check the Driveway

Take a few seconds to look at the driveway. Small cracks are fairly common. Often, those can be filled with a sealant. But bigger cracks, sinking slabs, flaking concrete surface (called *spalling*) can suggest more serious issues. You may want to contact a professional to discuss serious problems.

Walk Around the House

Look at the exterior of the home.

- Is paint flaking off from the house, around the windows or under the eaves?

- Are you seeing any cracks in the foundation of the home?

- Are there cracks in the mortar or the bricks?

- Is the siding still sound?

Inside – Cast Your Eyes in All Directions

Most people look at the flooring when they first walk into a house. That's understandable and smart. But many people stop there. We teach our clients to look up, look down and all around! Bad flooring can be replaced easily, though not inexpensively. However, the ceiling and the walls can be MUCH more expensive to repair/replace if there is damage or poor workmanship.

Walls and Ceilings

Look for:

- Poor drywall work on the seams of the sheetrock

- Poor patch work and painting on holes and dents

- Poor texturing on a ceiling repair

- Water damage

Is It Clean?

A dirty home is easy to spot. And you might say, "Not a big deal. We can get some soap and water and clean this place up." That's true. But a dirty home may tell you how the owners have treated the rest of the home.

The Kitchen

In the kitchen:

- Are the kitchen cabinets in good condition?

- Are kitchen cabinets solid wood or particleboard?

- Is there room for your kitchen table?

- Would you like a pantry?

Do-It-Yourself Work

Some home owners do a wonderful job of do-it-yourself (DIY) work. But we've toured LOTS of homes where the DIY'ers made it worse. If you know what to look for, you can usually spot the work of someone who did not know what they were doing. Look for:

- Sloppy painting

- Poor flooring job

- Poor drywall work

- Touch-up paint that does not match

- Holes in the wall have been carelessly filled, carelessly sanded and/or carelessly painted.

Check the Windows

Single-pane windows will cost you more money in both heating and cooling your home. Many older homes still have single pane windows. DEFINITELY do a window check as you tour a home. Ideally, the home you're interested in has double-pane windows.

The Furnace

Replacing the furnace can be a HUGE expense, so make sure that the furnace is in good condition. An inspector will help with this, and a furnace tech can give you a very good idea on the age and condition of the furnace. Typically, a furnace will last 15 to 20 years.

The Water Heater

The manufacturer's life expectancy of a water heater is about 8 to 12 years. That can vary with the location, quality of the unit and the quality of installation. Look for signs that you may need a new water heater:

- Rusting on the tank or in the water

- Failure to heat water

- Noises

- Leaks

Knock on Some Doors

Want an even better sense of the neighborhood? Go chat with several of the neighbors. Ask them about the neighborhood and the schools. Ask them if they like living there. You'll learn a lot!

Hire an Inspector

Be sure to hire an inspector to look at any home you're thinking about purchasing. He/she will be able to spot things you won't be able to see.

Take Notes and Photos

Bring a small notepad so you can take notes on what you did and didn't like in each home. Take some photos on your phone. After you've looked at several homes the details of each will begin to blur in your mind. The notes and photos will help!

CHAPTER 6

Frequently Asked Questions

Good Answers to Good Questions

I have never purchased a home. Where do I start?

The best place to begin is by figuring out how much you can afford. Within your budget, determine the loan amount you feel comfortable paying each month. Next, meet with a lender to get pre-approved. Then start following the Step-by-Step Checklist we've provided.

Does it cost me anything as a buyer to use a real estate agent?

No, typically the commissions for both real estate agents are covered by the seller of the home. That's one of the reasons we highly recommend you use an agent. Why not get all of his/her help if there's no cost to you? Pretty sweet, huh?

How can I find a great real estate agent?

Here are a couple of tips:

- Ask for suggestions from friends and family members you trust. They can tell you a lot.

- If you know the real estate agent's name, type it in Google and read his/her reviews.

- We suggest that you look at a few homes with an agent before you sign an agreement for him/her to serve as your agent. You'll have a better feel of his/her style and approach.

- Want some help? We provide a **free service** to help you find excellent agents in your area. We'll track down 2-3 excellent agents that get high recommendations. You can then contact the agents and select one that fits with your style.

How long does it take to buy a home?

It varies, depending upon the market. We've worked with buyers who have found their home on the first day out. Others have taken 3-4 months to find what they were looking for. Once you've signed a contract to purchase a home, it will take approximately 30 days from signing the contract to signing the final documents.

Does it cost me anything to meet with a lender and apply for a loan?

The requirements for each bank and lender vary. Some charge you an application fee. Others charge you for the credit report. To apply for a loan, you can pay anywhere from $0-$500.

How do I get the best interest rate?

You have to be careful here. Get a rate quote from several lenders. And ask them to explain the numbers. Putting more money down and having a credit score above 760 will help also.

Should I get my loan from a bank or a mortgage broker?

Talk with both. Choose whoever gives you the best rate with the lowest closing costs. Good insights are given in the *Definite Do's* section.

How can I spot poor workmanship in a home?

In our experience, most people focus more on the flooring than on the walls and ceilings when they tour a home. Flooring is LOTS easier to replace than poor construction and workmanship. As you walk through a home, look at the quality of workmanship. What is the condition of the paint and sheetrock? Is the concrete damaged? Are the ceilings cracked? Are the windows old and single-paned? If your agent can't help you spot these things, we'd encourage finding an agent who can.

How many homes should I walk through before deciding?

We've worked with clients who initially thought they wanted "this" from a home. But after visiting five or six homes, they realized they wanted "that." Your *Wish List* could "morph" after touring several homes. That's why we suggest checking out between five and ten homes before you lock in on one. Of course, you could always "stumble" onto an amazing home on the first round and love it.

What does a home inspector do?

The home inspection consists of a visual inspection and a written/electronic report of your property from top to bottom, including all the main systems (electrical, plumbing, furnace, AC, etc.). Some state laws and professional associations require home inspectors to give clients two documents as a matter of business and ethics: written home inspector contracts and written inspection reports. Request both from your inspector.

What is earnest money? And how much is needed?

Earnest money is used to show the seller that you are qualified and serious about buying the home. Depending upon the market and your location the earnest money can be from 1% to 3% of the home's purchase price. (Your agent will counsel you on this). That amount can climb higher in a competitive market. The money will likely be deposited in the escrow account of the seller's broker. That money will go toward the purchase of the home. You can lose your earnest money if you do not meet the deadlines specified in the contract. One of your agent's responsibilities is to keep you on task and safe from losing your earnest money.

CHAPTER 7

Real Estate Definitions

Simple Explanations for Terms That Sometimes Confuse

Appreciation: Expressing gratitude to your agent is always a good thing. But in real estate this term means something entirely different. In this context, it means an increase in value of your property as affected by external economic factors. For example, a person buys a home for $185,000 and, without doing any additional work on the home, sells it two years later for $215,000. The property would have "appreciated" $30,000.

Buyer Due Diligence: A buyer is granted a certain amount of time, negotiated by his/her agent, to investigate the home/property in order to determine if there are any serious concerns. During this time period a buyer can cancel the contract without any loss of earnest money.

Buyer's Market: This market condition happens when there are too many homes on the market and not enough buyers. So, the sellers cater to the buyers by dropping their prices and/or offering to pay closing costs (see "Closing Costs").

CC&Rs (Covenants, Conditions and Restrictions): These are the rules set forth by the various Homeowners Associations (see "Homeowners Association") that govern certain planned communities. The CC&Rs describe the requirements and limitations of what you can and cannot do with your property (e.g. whether or not you can put in a fence, have a pet, add on a shed, and so on). The main goal of the CC&Rs is to protect, preserve, and enhance property values in the community. Be sure you read these carefully before you buy a property that has CC&Rs.

Closing Costs: Closing costs usually add up to about 3% of the amount of your loan. If you are paying in cash your closing costs will be minimal (your title company can give you a good estimate). Closing costs are the fees you will pay to the following entities:

- Title company – for recording fees, title insurance, etc.

- The lender – for doing the work on your loan

- Appraiser

Closing on the Home: This term is often confused with Settlement (see *Definition*). Closing refers to the final transfer of the ownership of a house from the seller to the buyer. It occurs after all the terms of the contract have been met, payment has been received and the deed has been recorded.

Comparative Market Analysis (CMA): Also referred to as 'comps.' This is a report of similar homes in the area (usually within several miles) that were recently sold or are currently on the market. Though not as accurate as an appraisal, it will give you a "ballpark figure" of what the home is worth that you are buying or selling. Your real estate agent should provide this free of cost.

Concessions: Nope, these aren't refreshments for sale at the ballgame. Concessions are discounts or benefits offered (usually by the seller) to help lock in a real estate deal. These could include such things as cash back to the buyer, a reduction in sales price, or including a refrigerator. Most of the time concessions involve the seller agreeing to pick up a portion or all of the buyer's closing costs.

Conventional Loan: A conventional mortgage or conventional loan is any type of home buyer's loan that is not offered or secured by a government entity, such as the Federal Housing Administration (FHA), the U.S. Department of Veterans Affairs (VA) or the USDA Rural Housing Service. A conventional loan is available through a private lender (banks, credit unions, mortgage companies) or the two government-sponsored enterprises, the Federal National Mortgage Association (Fannie Mae) and the Federal Home Loan Mortgage Corporation (Freddie Mac).

Credit Report: A credit report is a summary of your financial dealings in paying your debts and other bills. This is not the same thing as a credit score.

Credit Score: A credit score is a three-digit numerical grade that is used to reflect your "credit worthiness." Although different types of credit scores exist, the FICO score is most common. FICO scores range from 300 to 850. The higher your score, the more likely lenders will be to trust that you'll pay back the money.

Down Payment: This is the amount of money required by the lender that you must put down to help qualify for a loan. A common misunderstanding is that the buyer must have at least 20% of the home price to put down on a loan. An FHA loan requires only 3.5% down. And many conventional loans require only 5% down.

Dual Agency (aka Limited Agency): This term means that your agent is representing both sides of the transaction. He/she represents both you and the seller. Why would he/she do that? To collect the commission on both sides of the transaction. Although it often works without problems we're not in favor of dual agency. Would you want a lawyer to represent you in a traffic accident if he is also representing the other party? We see it as a potential conflict of interest.

Earnest Money: An amount of money committed by the buyer to show the seller that he/she is earnest (serious) about the purchase. It is usually paid by check and is given to the buyer's real estate agent, who passes it on to the agent's brokerage. The check is cashed and held in escrow by the brokerage. The money goes toward the purchase of the home. This money can be lost to the seller if the buyer cancels the contract after certain deadlines have passed. But a good agent will do his/her utmost to guide you and prevent you from losing your earnest money.

Easement: The legal right granted to a person or entity to use someone's land for a specific purpose. For example, a utility company might have the right to dig up a section of your lawn to install a power cable. Or a neighbor may be given the right to drive onto your property to access his property.

Encroachment: When a property owner violates the property rights of his neighbor by building on or extending a structure (e.g. shed, fence, rock wall) onto a neighbor's property.

Encumbrance: This is a claim or a liability against a property. It includes such things as liens (see *Definition*), easements (see *Definition*), and encroachments (see *Definition*). An encumbrance can restrict the owner's ability to sell the property and transfer title (see *Definition*).

Equity: Home equity is the amount of money/value the homeowner has in a home. Equity can increase over time if the property value increases or the mortgage loan balance is paid down. For example, if Jason has put $55,000 into a $350,000 house and the house has increased in value by $10,000, Jason's home equity is $65,000 (the $55,000 he paid and $10,000 in increased value).

Escrow: Escrow in real estate usually refers to two situations. First, the buyer's earnest money is held by a bank or other financial institution in an escrow account until the transaction is completed. The money is applied toward the overall home sales price once the deal is finalized.

The second situation refers to the lender requiring the borrower to pay a specific amount each month for property taxes and home insurance. This money is put into an escrow account maintained by the lender. When the property tax and insurance bills are due, the lender pays them from the escrow account.

Exclusive Buyer Agent: This is an agent who has an allegiance only to you. His/her main job is to get you the best home at the best price. And here's the good news: You don't have to pay for his/her services. Really! The buyer's agent receives a commission from the seller – not from the buyer. So you should ALWAYS hire an agent to help you.

Exclusive Buyer-Broker Agreement: There is a wide variety of buyer broker agreements used throughout the United States. The most common buyer-broker agreement is between home buyers and real estate brokers (the owner of the agent's brokerage). This agreement outlines the obligations of the broker, the broker-agent relationship, and the responsibilities of the buyer for a specific time period (usually 3 to 6 months). With an "exclusive" agreement, the buyer cannot hire another broker to assist in the transaction. The agreement also lists the commission to be paid to the broker—even if the buyers find the house on their own. Make sure you read the agreement carefully and understand the terms and conditions.

Federal Housing Administration (FHA): The Federal Housing Administration is a United States government agency that sets standards for home construction and insures home loans made by banks and other private lenders.

Federal Housing Administration (FHA) Loan: This is a loan that is not *provided* by the federal government but is *insured* by the federal government, in case the home owner defaults on the loan. These loans tend to be at a lower interest rate because the government is insuring them. Popular with first-time homebuyers, FHA home loans require lower minimum credit scores and down payments than many conventional loans. FHA borrowers pay for mortgage insurance, which protects the lender from a loss if the borrower defaults on the loan.

Fiduciary Duties: When a real estate agent acts as an agent for a buyer or seller, he/she becomes a "fiduciary." With this relationship come certain legal duties, called "fiduciary duties," where the agent is expected to always act in the best interests of the client. Some of these duties included confidentiality, loyalty and obedience to the client.

Home Inspection: A buyer is NOT required to get an inspection of the home he/she is getting ready to purchase. But it is VERY UNWISE to skip this expense! The buyer pays for the inspection, usually at a cost of $200 to $400. But this inspection can save THOUSANDS OF DOLLARS by having an inspector determine critical issues BEFORE you buy the home. A good home inspection company will provide a report with photos of all areas of concern. The inspector should review this report with you, over the phone or in person, immediately after he has finished.

Homeowners' Association (HOA): This is a non-profit organization consisting of the homeowners who live in a planned community. The HOA makes and enforces rules for the properties within its jurisdiction. The purpose of the HOA is to protect the value of each other's property and to provide services to those in the community. If you purchase property within an HOA, you will be required to agree to abide by the CC&Rs (see

Definition). Be sure to read them carefully prior to your purchase. Most HOAs charge a monthly fee that you will be required to pay to receive the services offered (e.g. lawn care, snow removal, water, and sewer). Some HOAs can be very restrictive about what members can do with their properties. The HOA Board consists of members from the planned community who are elected to serve, without pay, to manage the financial affairs and enforce the CC&Rs.

Home Warranty: Typically, this is a *one-year policy*, paid for by the seller. It insures the home's crucial systems (plumbing, electrical, heating and AC) against failure. Depending on the comprehensiveness of the policy, it may also insure for the repair or replacement of such items as the oven, dishwasher, garbage disposal, and refrigerator. Buyers have the option to extend the warranty for additional years at their own expense.

Interest: This is the amount of money the lender charges you for borrowing money. When you get a mortgage, your interest payment is calculated as a percentage of the total loan amount. Let's say you have a 30-year $200,000 loan with a 4% interest rate. Your month to month payment would amount to about $955. Part of that monthly payment would go toward paying back what you borrowed, the "principal,", and the rest would go toward interest. Over 30 years, you would end up paying back not only $200,000, but an extra $143,739 in interest.

Interest Rate: This is the percent that the lender charges you on the money you have borrowed to purchase the home. Check with several lenders to see what their interest rates are. They can vary considerably.

Lien: This is a notice attached to a property stating that a creditor is owed money. For example, if the homeowner never fully pays a contractor for finishing the basement, the contractor can put a lien on the property. It gives the unpaid party a legal claim to a portion of the property. Typically, the owner is not able to sell or refinance a property until a lien is cleared.

Loan-to-Value (LTV): Loan-to-Value or LTV is the percent of money you're borrowing of the home's value. If the home is valued at $350,000 (as determined by an appraiser) and you're borrowing $300,000, your loan-to-value is about 86%.

Low Ball Offer: This means you are offering MUCH lower than you should for the price of the home. Don't go there. A low ball offer usually makes the sellers and their agent angry. Don't try to take advantage of the other party. Go for "win-win" transactions. Work to make it fair for both parties. You'll sleep better and make lots more friends.

Multiple Listing Service (MLS): This is online service that contains all the specifics about a home, including price, address, age, square footage, number of bedrooms, number of baths, etc. Only homes listed by real estate agents are entered in the MLS. A real estate agent pays a monthly fee to belong to this service, so homes that are not represented by an agent (e.g. for sale by owner) are not included in the MLS.

Mortgage Brokerage: This is an independent company that works with numerous lenders throughout the country. It is not a bank or a credit union. Mortgage brokerages do not fund the loan but seek to match the buyer with lenders who best match the buyer's situation (e.g. good credit, bad credit, etc.).

PITI: This is an abbreviation pertaining to a mortgage. It refers to the **P**rincipal (amount borrowed), **I**nterest, property **T**axes, and homeowners' **I**nsurance.

Points: Mortgage points are also known as discount points. These are fees paid to the lender in exchange for a reduction in the interest rate. One point costs 1% of your mortgage amount (i.e. $1,000 for every $100,000).

Pre-Approved: Pre-approved is similar to pre-qualified. However, pre-approval usually requires more documentation and verification of your income, assets, and debts. It's a higher level of qualification. And it often requires a credit check, which will result in a hard inquiry (one that affects your credit score) on your credit report.

Pre-Approval Letter: This is a letter created by your lender that states how much money you have been approved to receive in the purchase of your home. The letter can be sent to you or your agent. Many sellers will require a pre-approval or pre-qualification letter.

Pre-Qualified: This is sometimes confused with "pre-approved." It is not the same thing. Pre-qualification is a similar process to pre-approval but requires less documentation.

Principal: This is the amount of money you borrow to buy your home. If you purchase a $200,000 home with a 10% down payment of $20,000, your principal is $180,000. This is the amount you will need to pay back, plus interest.

Private Mortgage Insurance (PMI): Private mortgage insurance is a monthly insurance premium paid by the buyer to the lender to protect the lender if the buyer is not able to pay the mortgage. Once the buyer reaches 20% equity in the home, the PMI should be discontinued. If not, call the lender and ask for it to be discontinued. If you put down at least 20% on your down payment, you will not be required to pay for PMI.

> NOTE: *Although you can cancel private mortgage insurance, you cannot cancel Federal Housing Administration insurance. You can get rid of FHA insurance by refinancing into a conventional loan.*

Real Estate Agent: A real estate agent is a professional who has earned a real estate license in his/her state. Earning a license usually requires completion of a minimum number of classes and a test, though requirements vary by state. Agents work under the supervision of a broker.

Real Estate Broker: These brokers are usually managers or owners of a real estate agency and have agents working under them as salespeople. They must take additional real estate classes and pass a test. They also pay additional fees to maintain their state-issued broker license.

Realtor: A Realtor is a licensed real estate salesperson who belongs to the State and National Association of Realtors®. Realtors are held to a higher ethical standard than licensed agents and agree to adhere to a Code of Ethics. All Realtors are real estate agents but not all real estate agents are Realtors.

Seller Disclosures: A document with a series of questions the seller must answer to disclose (reveal) any significant problems that once existed or currently exist on the property.

Seller's Market: A seller's market occurs when the demand for homes exceeds the available supply. Because the number of homes is limited, the sellers often receive multiple offers – which cause the home cost to rise.

Settlement: This is often confused with *Closing* (see *Definition*). Settlement takes place when both parties sit down with their title companies or attorneys and sign the documents that will transfer the property from seller to buyer upon closing.

Short Sale: The word "short" has nothing to do with time. It refers to owners who "come up short" on the money they owe on their home. Specifically, the owners owe more on their mortgage than the home is currently worth. For example, when the real estate "bubble" burst in 2007-08, many homeowners found their home value had dropped below what they owed on their home. A short sale occurs when a homeowner's lender allows the homeowner to sell the house for less than the amount owed on the mortgage. No matter what you've heard, buying a short sale home can be a long and complicated process.

Title: People often confuse the term "title" with "deed." A deed is a legal document used to confirm the ownership rights to a property. It is written document signed by both the buyer and the seller. The title is not a document but rather a concept that states you have the rights to a property.

Title Company: A title company plays a critical role in the purchase/sale of a home. The title company:

1. Conducts a title search to see if the seller is the legitimate owner with the rights to sell the property.

2. Determines if there are any liens against the property (unpaid taxes, HOA fees, etc.)

3. Issues title insurance for the buyer and lender, protecting them against any claims with the property.

4. Obtains signatures on all of the closing documents.

5. Receives and distributes payments relating to the transaction.

6. Insures that the necessary documents have been prepared and recorded to transfer title to the new owner.

7. The final closing for a home is typically held at the office of the title company.

Different states and areas vary as to whether the seller or buyer (or both) select and pay for title company services. Your real estate agent can answer questions regarding the policy in your area.

Title Insurance: This is an insurance policy purchased by the buyer through the title company that protects the buyer if any party claims to have ownership in the property the buyer has just purchased.

Title Commitment: Prior to the issuance of title insurance (see Definition), an extensive title search is made of public records regarding the history of ownership of a property, including liens (see *Definition*), encroachments (see *Definition*) and encumbrances (see *Definition*). The title commitment is exactly what it says: a commitment to provide title insurance to the lender and the buyer under the described terms. The title commitment also outlines the conditions and any exceptions that will impact the title insurance policy.

CHAPTER 8

Helpful Resources

Check Out the Free Help and Info Below

Free Government Tips and Information

Find clear, impartial answers to hundreds of financial questions at: Consumer Financial Protection Bureau

https://www.consumerfinance.gov/

Nationwide Financial Assistance Programs

Search these terms in

- The Chenoa Fund:

https://staging-chenoafundcom.kinsta.com/providing-down-payments-on-fha-and-conventional-loan/

- The Dream Maker

https://penfedfoundation.org/apply-for-assistance/dream-makers/?content=on

- USDA Single Family Direct Loan

  https://www.rd.usda.gov/programs-services/single-family-housing-direct-home-loans

- USDA Single Family Guaranteed Loan

  https://www.rd.usda.gov/programs-services/single-family-housing-guaranteed-loan-program

- Veterans Administration Home Loan

  https://www.benefits.va.gov/homeloans/

Credit Report Information

The three major credit bureaus are:

- Equifax: *www.equifax.com*
- Experian: *www.experian.com*
- Transunion: *www.transunion.com*

Credit reporting agencies are required to provide consumers with one free credit report every twelve months. See:

> *https://www.annualcreditreport.com/yourRights.action.*

For additional information about credit reports go to:

> *www.ftc.gov.*

Community Resources

1. Shopping and entertainment: **WalkScore.com**
2. School ratings: **GreatSchools.org**
3. Crime statistics: **CrimeReports.com, NeighborhoodScout.com, SpotCrime.com**
4. Public transportation: **APTA.com**

Mortgage Resources

- **FHA Loans**: Borrowers can qualify for loans with as little as 3.5% down: **FHA.com**

- **USDA**: The US Department of Agriculture operates a home loan assistance program. You don't have to be a farmer or live on a farm. The program focuses on rural areas and allows up to 100% financing by giving guarantees to lenders: **RD.USDA.gov**

- **Good Neighbor Next Door**: The US Department of Housing and Urban Development (HUD) sponsors this program, which was originally called the *Teacher Next Door Program*. It was later expanded to include emergency medical technicians, law enforcement and firefighters. It allows 50% discounts off the list price of homes located in revitalization areas. You must live in the property for at least three years.

- **VA Loans**: The US Department of Veterans Affairs helps veterans, surviving spouses and service members buy homes with no down payment or mortgage insurance:

  Benefits.VA.gov/homeloans/

Want Free Help?

Services We Offer Free of Charge

We offer free help with:

- Locating excellent lenders in your area.

- Finding great real estate agents in your area.

- Locating any housing grants or assistance available in your city, county or state.

Check out our ABOUT US page for contact information.

Favor Request

If you liked our book and found it helpful we would appreciate your kind review on Amazon.

Thanks!

All our best!

Tim and Clint

About Us

Timothy L Carver

Tim Carver has been a professional educator for 37 years. He is a real estate agent with *Jody Deamer and Company* in Ogden, Utah.

He is a published author and has written a weekly real estate column in a local newspaper.

Tim has completed special training in helping clients find long-term investment properties. He also has experience in building and remodeling, along with developing and selling subdivisions.

Tim is happily married, has two children and six grandchildren. He loves to spend time with family and with golf buddies.

He can be reached at 801-458-1048 or *tlcarver@comcast.net*.

JODY DEAMER & COMPANY
a full-service real estate brokerage

Clint T Carver

Clint Carver has worked in architectural and engineering firms.

He has both a real estate license and a mortgage license. He currently works as a mortgage officer for *Beam Lending* in Layton, Utah, where he is consistently recognized as one of the top performers.

He is also a professional photographer, graphic artist and web designer.

He is happily married and has three children (and a cat and dog who are convinced they own the family home).

He can be reached at 801-784-3927 or *clintcarver3@gmail.com*.

Individual NMLS #8753442 - Company NMLS #1104582

Made in the USA
Middletown, DE
11 September 2019